MAKENI
HOMEBOYS

K.A MULENGA

© Kalenga Augustine Mulenga

Makeni Homeboys

Published by Kalenga Augustine Mulenga
Johannesburg, South Africa
augustine@kamulenga.com

ISBN: 978-0-7961-4074-6
eISBN: 978-0-7961-4075-3

2 4 6 8 10 9 7 5 3 1

Layout and cover design by Boutique Books

CONTENTS

CONTENTS

INTRODUCTION

Makeni! To this day, I have no idea what 'Makeni' means or where it got its name from, but what I do know is that it is where I grew up, where I became a man, where I met my wife, where I learned how to ride a bike... the list is endless.

This book is about friendships, basketball, and the strong bond a sport can create; and, of course, it is about Makeni - a farm area in the southern part of Lusaka, the capital of Zambia. It is about friendships that no distance can sepa- rate, friendships that were forged from playing basketball. This is no ordinary sports story about winning and losing, or about being cheered on by our parents. Actually, none of our parents ever came to watch us play, and my mum has never seen me take a jump shot (okay, that is not true. I recently sent out a video of me taking and scoring two jump shots, here is the link) https://clipchamp. com/watch/r2TloD9a8Nq Sit back and enjoy the ride!

Makeni Homeboys.

① THE EARLY DAYS

I was born on the 5th of September 1975, in a small town called Luanshya in the Copperbelt Province of Zambia. From what I have been told, we moved to Makeni when I was a baby and lived in Plot 80. Even though I do not know what Makeni means, I do know it is a close-knit community where everyone knows each other's names and people look out for each other.

My late father, Kelvin Goodwin Mlenga, was the first Black African editor of the Zambia Daily Mail. Years later, he switched careers and worked for Roan Consolidated Copper Mines as a Company Secretary. However, when I was seven years of age, he died while working for Zambia Consolidated Copper Mines. He died on his way back from a work trip from the Copperbelt.

My father's first wife was a Zimbabwean lady whom I unfortunately never met because she died before I was conceived. He had three children with her, namely Priscilla, Tulani and Bertha. She died in Ndola in 1972, when my dad was only forty years old and my siblings were eight, four, and three. They were very young to lose a mother.

A few years later, my dad met my mum in Ndola and they got married in August 1974. When they got married, my mum had already had a son, my brother, Clement, from a previous romantic relationship. He was four years old when my parents got married. They became a blended family and decided to add to their blood, and that is when I was born.

At the time I was born, we were living at 2 Mzee Kenyatta Road, off Ngumbo Road, in between State House and Longacres Shopping Centre. My dad purchased a farm in Makeni and we moved there in early 1976.

We all went to the International School of Lusaka, except Priscilla who attended the Dominican Convent, which changed its name to St Mary's in her last year of school in 1980 when it became partially funded and controlled by the government.

At the time my mother met my dad, she was working as a secretary at Jacks and Partners, a legal firm where the late President of Zambia, Mr. Levy Mwanawasa, used to work. But, when she got married, she became a full-time housewife and a stay-at-home mum. This was the norm in the olden days, so it was not a surprise at all.

Working for ZCCM (Zambia Consolidated Copper Mines), my dad's job as company secretary was an important position, and he was well-known by the President, Dr. Kenneth Kaunda. This worked in his favour, and he had many benefits, including access to the company's cars, housing allowances, and fees paid for by the company. We used to be driven to school by company drivers. Therefore, the unexpected death of my father was a huge loss to my mum and us, his children, but it also had a significant impact on our financial standing. There was some life cover, but most of it went to pay the mortgage.

When it comes to celebrating birthdays, our family tradition is peculiar. I witnessed this when I turned seven years of age. We prepare dinner and sing a birthday song, *Happy Birthday*, cut the cake and opened presents. Unfor- tunately, the peculiarity of this birthday was that my dad never came back from work and we thought that perhaps he was running late. As we waited for him, we heard a hoot at the gate and one of my brothers opened it, and in drove Auntie Stella Mwenso and some of her kids. We called her Auntie Stella because of the huge age gap between us, but she was actually our first cousin. Her mother was Dad's immediate elder sister. She and her brother, Peter, had been orphans from a tender age and had been raised by Dad.

She was wailing, and then my mum and sisters followed suit. My brothers were just shaking their heads in shock. My sister, Bertha, was screaming, holding a picture of my dad to her chest. Obviously, I was very confused. I was but just a seven-year-old who wanted to eat his birthday cake and open his presents.

The next thing I knew, we were all bundled into several cars and taken to the Mwenso's house in Roma, Lusaka. No one explained to me what had happened until the day of his burial. My sister, Priscilla, took me aside and explained it to me, using a Bible story. I cannot remember which one it was, but it fulfilled its goal and I ended up understanding. His death, however, only hit home when it came time for the body viewing. My dad was not moving and was in a coffin. His eyes were closed, and that is when I finally realised that he was gone and not coming back.

The next few years were a bit of a blur. Mum had to make a plan to make ends meet. She had five mouths to feed and educate. My brothers were transferred to Mpelembe Secondary School, a ZCCM-sponsored school in Kitwe, a town in the Copperbelt. They were given scholarships due to my dad's high standing and position. This eased the burden of paying school fees at ISL (International School of Lusaka). Priscilla was at the University of Zambia, studying psychology, and Bertha and I stayed at ISL.

Before I knew it, Bertha moved to Zimbabwe and so did Tulani. He didn't fit in at Mpelembe. Clement completed his Grade 12 at Mpelembe and I left ISL in 1989.

I always wondered how my friends and I all ended up playing basketball. We all went to different schools (except for Evans Sodala). The other thing that surprised me was that Zambia was not a basketball country. The national sport is soccer and it is what my country has achieved the most in. I cannot remember what made me fall in love with the game, I was relatively short and short-sighted and used to have to play with my glasses on. As you would have guessed, I broke so many pairs of glasses. To add to the list, not only did my mum have to replace them but she also had to fork out cash at least twice a year for new sneakers.

I started playing basketball at the International School of Lusaka, I cannot remember the exact year but it was definitely in primary school, around Grade 5 or 6. ISL, as it was called, had four basketball courts and another indoor court was built when I was still there, to begin with. Now, this was something, since indoor courts were rare in Zambia.

This is a brief background of how and when I fell in love with the sport.

② THE PLAYERS

Here is a list of the friends and players who ended up being more like brothers than friends are:

1. Nicholas Chitulangoma aka Nikolai
2. Innocent Chitulangoma aka Ice T
3. Mumba Bwakya aka Vop Daze
4. Kennedy Kapaya aka Super Ken aka Rumper
5. Evans Sodala aka Badala aka Barkley
6. Kunda Mapipo aka Kundie B
7. George Zulu
8. Wezi Mtonga aka Buzz
9. Kazhila Mambwe aka Kazhi Babe
10. Victor Makai
11. Brian Makai aka Mbonge Brown
12. Sydney Kozhi Makai
13. Obierrah aka Big Joe
14. Kamima Nyirenda
15. Tumundila Kazunga aka Tum
16. And of course, me aka Kal

All of the above lived in Makeni, and even though some may have moved away but we remained Homeboys.

Most of us had elder brothers who also played basket- ball. We all looked up to them and dreamed of emulating them. Names like Francis and Alex Makai, and Musonda Kapaya, were superstars of our time and we used to boast that we used to play with them.

③
THE COURTS

The main court was based at a place called *Makeni Ecumenical Centre*, where we used to hit a nearby Anglican Church's windows with basketball balls.

To my surprise, none of the windows broke from those hits. I am guessing God wanted us to keep playing there because it kept us out of mischief!

The court at the Ecumenical Centre was not of the best standard. The rim was made of thick metal and there were no nets on the rim at all. At half time, when you needed a drink of water, you had to walk more than three hundred metres from the court. And this was the closest tap.

In the beginning, our elder brothers dominated the game and passed it on to us, as we grew older. We stepped into their shoes.

At the centre, a caretaker always gave us a hard time when we wanted to play basketball, but with much convincing and pleading, he would cave in.

The distance was never an issue for us to play. During school holidays, we would all meet up at the centre and play from 2 pm until it got too dark to see. This was a weekend ritual without fail.

Another thing I remember is carrying a hand pump to the court because the balls would never see out the game and we would have to pump it at least four times for us to continue with the game.

As our games advanced, we needed to move on to better courts and even though the Islamic Centre's court was far from home for most of us, it did not stop us from playing there.

The walk was something we would savour with all the stories, jokes, laughter, and excitement about another game of basketball!

Another thing that basketball taught us was oneness. The Islamic Centre's courts were at the local Mosque and there was a school and a clinic as well. However, no one used the basketball courts except us. So, when the rims got rusty and fell off, the onus was on us to fix them.

You have to remember that none of us was working; we solely depended on our parents for pocket money. We would collate the money to take out the backboard and get the rim welded back on, using one of our parent's cars to transport them to and from the welder, and then back to the Islamic Centre. How's that for commitment!?

Another project that we entered into enthusiastically was putting up a board and rim at the local primary school called *Bayuni*. This school had no wall or barrier or fence around it and it had a piece of concrete slab or tarmac that was not utilised. We approached the school board and asked for permission to put up the hoop and it was granted without any fuss. Their approval was one easy thing, but living up to our words was another thing. That is when the hard part began, the execution. Evans and Kennedy ran the project; getting together the materials for the board and the rim and looking for a pole to attach the board to. This project took ages, about two-to-three years.

Unfortunately, it never took off until I had started working and all of us had other commitments.

Today, I have no idea what happened to that half-court, and even though it was not a success, it brought us together in trying to achieve a common goal.

④
THE CHITULANGOMA'S

Nicholas was born in 1974, and Innocent was born in 1976. In between was my birth. These brothers were my closest friends and we were closer as well, geographically. Our farms were next to each other and back in our days, there were no walls or fences surrounding the properties. We would literally just walk into our neighbour's yard.

Even though we were closer, my friends had different personalities. For instance, Nicholas is humble, laid back, and a virtual genius. On the other hand, Innocent is outgoing, liked by everybody, and a happy-go-lucky person.

When it came to basketball, though, they were both lethal and passionate about the game.

Nicholas and I were in the same grade in high school, he was at Chasa Boys in the Eastern Province, while I was at Namwianga Christian Secondary School in Kalomo, Southern Province. So, we finished high school in the same year, 1991.

While waiting for our matric results, which meant we had more time to kill together, we would reserve our morn- ings for a club-and-ball sport, golf. We carved out three holes in the farm with only eight irons, a sand wedge, a putter, and about four balls, we would play those three holes throughout the morning.

And as convinced as we were about our matric results because it was now months since we have been waiting, we came up with an idea to look for a basketball club that we could join. We were young and ambitious. We decided to join Profound Hurricanes, a team that was sponsored by the National Provident Fund (NPF). The training was from 3 pm to 5 pm, from Tuesday to Friday with games on Saturdays. To get to the training, we would have to get on a minibus to town and walk to the NPF head office. There we would get on a sponsored bus along with the netball players Most, if not all, of the other players, were much older than us and used to work for the NPF, so we were naturally overwhelmed. However, this did not dampen our spirits. After training, the bus would drop most of the players near their respective homes and we were dropped at Makeni Filling Station. We would get on a minibus and drop off at the Ecumenical Centre, usually around 17:45. We would peep in to see some of the younger players playing and being semi-pros, we would walk in as proud as peacocks and play until sunset, around 19:00.

That was our routine. In the morning, it was golf; in the afternoon, it was training with the Hurricanes;

and early in the evening, it was a game or two at the Ecumenical Centre. Our energy levels were insane and we never grew weary of this routine. Also, we never ran out of things to talk about. Even after a session during the week or a weekend game in the league, we would get back home and chat for another hour or two before seeing each other again the next morning Innocent was in his final year of school that year, so we would only see him over the school holidays.

Eventually, the Grade 12 results came out and Nicholas was accepted at the University of Zambian, where he played for the Unza Pacers, who were part of the Zambia Basketball Association, in the same league as the Hurricanes.

I, on the other hand, moved on to Chingola in the Copperbelt to study Accounting at the Chingola School of Accounts. I joined the team called *Nchanga*, which was not too far from the College, and one of the seniors, the late Mwenya Munkonge, showed me the ropes.

Nicholas and I lost touch for a while because from Chin- gola, I moved to Zamim in Lusaka, and I was in the UK for a year. Later, I went to Ndola for a year and started work, and then eventually, I relocated to South Africa, in 1999.

Today, we are still in touch over Facebook and I was happy to meet him at Makeni Mall in **2019** I was in a queue at the ATM. It was as if we had seen each other yesterday! The same could be said about Innocent, he worked for one of the 5-star hotels, he attended Zamim after I had left there, relocated to the Eastern Province for a short period, and later, he relocated to the US. He is still in the US and we communicate via Facebook from time to time.

⑤
MUMBA BWAKYA

Mumba aka Vop Daze. What a unique nick-name for a unique person. Mumba lived across the street from our house. He was a couple of years younger than I was and we were not that close in the beginning because of the small age gap, as well as the difference in school levels. Growing up, Mumba was short for his age and we were all under the impression that he would stay that height forever! We were all proven wrong, he had a growth spurt. Actually, he is slightly taller than I am now!

I can remember learning to ride a bike with him on our dusty road. Makeni only had gravel roads in our area; only the main road leading to town was tarmac. This was before we started playing basketball together. My memory of our first linkup on the court is sketchy, to say the least. I can't recall how he came to start playing basketball with us as he was very small in stature compared to the rest of us.. However, Mumba was a great addition to the team. He was enthusiastic and would always start the game with extreme energy, but alas, as the game would wear on his energy would dissipate. Actually, that is where the name Vop came from. It was Pov spelled backward. Pov refers to the bubbles that are formed when hand-washing powder is put in a bucket of water. The foam that is formed from shaking the water is called *Pov*. However, after some time the foam bubbles dissipate.

Mumba was the first-born boy and his brother, fondly known as Papa, was much younger than he was. Because of this, Pov had access to the family van, a white Peugeot, that we named Gra-Gra because of the noise its engine would make when idling.

Mumba saved us a lot of energy walking to the courts to play because we would all pile into the back of Gra-Gra and make our way to the Islamic Courts or sometimes even play against other neighbourhood teams at different locations. Our friendship was based on proximity, but also on our shared interests namely basketball and music.(After I started work and basketball took a back seat, Mumba was at college and we continued to hang out together, usually joined by our tall but non-basketball-playing friend Mailon Moono. When I relocated to South Africa, we kept in contact and whenever I would visit Zambia, we would get together for old times' sake.

We are still in touch on Facebook and he even wanted a sneak look at this book before it was finished!

⑥

KENNEDY KAPAYA

This book is in memory of Kennedy Kapaya aka Super Ken or Rumper. He died this year(2021) and I am still shocked and saddened by this.

What a player... what a friend!

Kennedy was a late bloomer in terms of basketball. Most of us started playing basketball either in late primary or early secondary school. He started late into secondary school and became better than all of us! We actually taught him the basics at the Ecumenical Centre. I remember when he was still in his school uniform and his first shot almost cleared the wall. To cut a long story short, he took to the game as a duck takes to water. He was a deadly three-point shooter and he had a leap like no one I knew. He could slam dunk with power and was an excellent defensive player as well. His favourite player was Michael Jordan and he tried to copy everything he did, even his signature wagging tongue. Kennedy became obsessed with the game, collecting jerseys, videotapes and trying to play every day if possible. He even put up a backboard and rim in his dusty yard.

Having a half court in the driveway or backyard may be commonplace in America but in Zambia, let alone a farm- house in Makeni, such a thing was unheard of. All this from a person who had never touched a basketball until his mid-late teens!

Not only did I respect Kennedy as a player, but also as a person. He was an orphan and had to look after his younger brothers. He had to pay his way through school and his money was made from renting out a cottage on the property and from farm produce.

As a result, we became close and much time was spent in his room watching Come Fly With Me, a Michael Jordan documentary, or Michael Jordan Above and Beyond.

Kennedy was a Parent's dream and all our parents loved him because of his maturity and discipline. And I would use that advantage whenever we wanted to go out. Mum would ask if Kennedy would be there, and if the answer was 'yes', then we were granted permission to go out. If the answer was 'no', then permission would not be granted.

Like with all the others, when I relocated, we lost touch and he did not have a Facebook page, but whenever I would go to Zambia, even if it was just for the weekend, he would make an effort to come see me. We would talk for hours like we used to, in the olden days.

When our friend, Evans, sent me a message this year, informing me of Kennedy's passing, I was devastated. You are greatly missed, my friend. MHSRIP!

⑦

EVANS SODALA

This person was the main reason I moved from the International School of Lusaka, a school where diplomats' kids and expatriates from all over the world went, a school where we could go dressed in anything we liked to, to Namwianga Christian Secondary School in Kalomo. Kalomo is a tiny town in the Southern Province of Zambia.

From that, I am guessing you can tell how close we were. The term childhood friend is exactly what Evans is to me, to this day. *Where to start...*

If I am not mistaken, our families knew each other since the 1980s. His family moved out of Makeni but came back and stayed there until the late 1990s. Our elder brothers were also friends, not to the same degree as we were, though. Evans and I shared the same passion for basketball and movies. I remember watching three-to-four movies a day during the school holidays. His dad owned video stores across the Southern Province, so movies were always in good supply.

Basketball-wise, Evans was not the tallest but he had a sweet three-point shot. He could also use his strength against much taller opposition. His catchphrase was LIMBA. Simply put, it means you have to be strong.

In 1989, I moved to Namwianga, for Grade 10. Evans and I were not in the same dorm or the same class, and we would have our vicissitudes as friends. This trend continued even after school but as the phrase goes, "We rode out the storm and we are still close to this day."

After Namwianga, Evans went to England, Birmingham, to begin his law degree. He would come for holidays once a year and would always bring basketball video tapes and the latest NBA jerseys (Michael Jordan, Shawn Kemp to name a few).

One time, I met up with him when I was in the UK and spent the weekend at his university. He didn't expect me at all, I remember calling him from a public telephone, letting him know that I was calling him from Oxford Street in London. He was dumbfounded! He gave me his address together with its how-to get there. Three days later, I was on a coach to Birmingham.

In 2005, when I got married, Evans, Mumba, and Kennedy attended my wedding in Lusaka. This shows how close we were and how far back we go.

He is now married and a qualified lawyer. We chat via WhatsApp and Facebook messenger.

8

KUNDA MAPIPO

Kundie B, the gentle giant. He and Kennedy had the deepest voices among us. He was a very calm character and frankly, I have never seen him upset.

Kunda was one of our prospects but he didn't quite work out. He had the physique and height of a basketball player, yet he could not get the basics right: Bouncing, dribbling, and simple jump shots. He did try though and I can definitely applaud him for that.

One thing we did have in common was music! We would sit for hours going through each other's music collection. Back in those days, original audio-cassette tapes were hard to come by, so we would wait for the kids who went to school in England to come for their summer holidays and raid their collections. Either we would record all the songs via a double-cassette recorder at his house or at my house, then return them back to the UK-bound people once we were done.

The other thing we had in common was that his parents and my mum were close. We were all

Catholics (come to think of it, so many families in Makeni were Catholic!), but only Kunda, Nicholas, and I were regulars at mass on Sunday.

These were good days when drinking and smoking was the furthest thing from our minds. It was all about basketball and music and for the latter, my definite partner in crime was Kunda!

I haven't seen Kunda since I relocated. From what I have heard, he works for Zesco, the state-owned electricity supply company in Zambia. He is married with twins and the last time I spoke to him was in 2010. Kunda was a very focused and humble person and I always knew he would be successful in life. I wasn't wrong!

9

GEORGE ZULU, KAMIMA NYIRENDA, AND WEZI MTONGA

I put these three people together because of their prox- imity to each other. They all lived relatively close to each other and relatively closer to the Islamic Centre than most of us.

George was tall and lanky. He also had a passion for the game, but he never took it as seriously as Kennedy did. He only played local Makeni basketball to the best of my knowledge and didn't join any of the clubs in the Zambia Basketball Association (ZBA). He always used to come to play with his Parents' light truck and with his little brother, Maya, and his little cousin (I can't remember his name).

One thing was certain, though: Every Sunday, George, Maya, and little cousin would always be there and would only miss out for a very good reason.

We are friends on Facebook but that is as far as it goes. Kamima was also tall by Zambian standards. He liked basketball and was an occasional player, but he was not one of the week-in and week-out kind of players. As a person, he was nice and had a good attitude. Today, I can see why he is a Zambia Airforce General, and as Evans told me, he is a highly trained pilot who flies the President. He has been to China, the USA, and France for training. He brought the Presidential Gulf Stream to Zambia. One of only three pilots in Zambia who can fly it.

One of the success stories from the Makeni Homeboys! I haven't communicated with him at all since back in those days. I wish him all the best, and I am very proud of him. Wezi aka Buzz! This was another character of note! Our families go way back. He got his nickname from Bosley, from Charlie's Angels. His elder brother and sisters were close to my elder brothers and sisters. In fact, we were related. His late mum was the first cousin to my maternal grandfather (my mum's late father). Of his two elder brothers, only one of them used to play basketball as well, but not like we did. Wezi went to Canisius Secondary School, a Catholic school in the same province as Namwianga (the school Evans and me attended). Canisius and Namwianga were powerhouses in the Southern Province, so you would expect Wezi to be just as passionate about the game as Evans and I. But that was not the case, Wezi loved the good life and after completing Grade 12, he qualified to attend the University of Zambia (UNZA). Wezi and

I had many adventures during this transition in both our lives, but they are not basketball related, so I will leave you to let your imagination run wild as to what these adventures entailed. He didn't finish his degree at UNZA, he moved on to the UK, studied and worked there and eventually moved back to Zambia. We communicate via Facebook here and there.

Chapter 10: Kazhila Mambwe and Obierrah Kazhy Babe and Obierrah were both good players, but we did not have a close friendship. To prove that, I didn't even know Obierrah's surname.

I will start with Kazhila. He lived just up the road from me. On the court, though, Kazhila was a good player. He didn't take his game any further than Makeni, but he did have a growth spurt when we were teenagers. So, he had a bit of an advantage on us.

Currently, Kazhila resides in Lusaka and works for the Building Society. I haven't seen or communicated with him since the late 1990s.

As mentioned above, Obierrah and I were not close at all. I think Obierrah was from Uganda (or somewhere in East Africa). Naturally, he was well built without having to lift any weights, and he was a good height for basketball. Also, he had a quiet demeanour. He used to live extremely far from most of us and would always make an effort to come and play on weekends. Kennedy aptly gave him the nickname *Big Joe* due to his size. That's about all we knew about him, and to this day, I have no idea where he is and what he is doing.

I included these people because of their commitment to the Homeboys, and when it comes to friendship, that's another story.

⑩
THE MAKAIS

What a sporting family! Where do I start! I will list the male members of the family, as my memory of the females is fuzzy:

1. Eugene Makai
2. Alex Makai
3. Francis Makai
4. Fred Makai
5. Victor Makai
6. Brian Makai
7. Sydney Makai

Of these seven, Eugene and Fred were not basketball players. However, Victor used to play with us, but he never took it further (at school or at a club after school) Alex and Francis were both players for ZBA(**Zambia Basketball Association, which at the time had 10 clubs)**) and were much older than us. They were our heroes. Francis was one of the best players of his time.

So, I will not get into details with them since they were not part of our clique.

I will start with Brian. He was a passionate player and was sensitive as well. The Makais were all-tall and had incredible physiques so that helped Brian play power forward. Brian and I were in the same grade at high school. He went to Kafue Boys, a town not far from Lusaka. We never met at the high school level. Our times on the court were mainly at the Ecumenical Centre and a few times at the Islamic Centre. This was because his family moved from Makeni to Lusaka West. It was a loss to the Homeboys and we would still bump into each other at ZBA games. Also, we came up against each other in a neighbourhood battle (Makeni versus Lusaka West), but more on that later. Currently, he is in Thailand and I see from his Facebook page that he still plays, which is very impressive. We still keep contact on Facebook.

Sydney was the last born in the Makai family. He was a skinny-little kid when we used to play at the Ecumenical Centre, and at the time we had no idea that he would have a major growth spurt and would end up being one of the best players in Zambia. The huge advantage that he had was that when he was smaller, he had a lower sense of gravity, which would allow him to dribble with speed. Also, as a point guard or shooting guard, he had a good three-point shot. After the growth spurt, he could play centre or forward. A dribbling, three-point shooting, dunking, aggressive player and a defenders nightmare!

Due to our age gap, we were not that close, and we never got to play that much together due to his family relocating before his growth spurt. Today, Sydney is a doctor and lives in America. We communicate on Facebook here and there.

(11)

TUMUNDILA KAZUNGA

I have known Tum for as long as I can remember. Our late fathers were good friends, and our mothers are still close. His elder brothers were extremely close with my two elder brothers. The thing about our friendship, Tum and I, is that to this day, we are close and the last time he was in South Africa, he spent the night at my house. Of all the Homeboys, he is the only one who has been to my house and spent time with my family. I am sure you get the picture!

Tum's dad was appointed as a diplomat in the 1980s. As a result, they moved away from Zambia when he was young. They moved to Belgium and Sweden, and I guess he learned how to play basketball in one of those countries. Whenever he would be back in Zambia, on either a vacation or one of his other missions, he would join us to play. I remember Nicholas and I invited him once to play for the Hurricanes because we were short of players. For him, this was the closest he got to playing professional basketball! He had a good height for the game and we enjoyed playing with him.

As I mentioned earlier, Tum was always on the move and he moved to England in the 1990s. When my mum sent me to the UK to complete my accounts, I stayed with him. He was working full-time and I was at college. It was a great time, two young men living together and I will forever be grateful to him for showing me how to get around, since it was my first time going overseas.

When I moved back to Zambia and started working, Tum would be in and out of the country, and we would always go out and even when I relocated to South Africa and was living on my own, he came to spend a weekend with me.

He is married now with two kids and living in London. This friendship is one of a kind, it stood the test of time and the only glitch in it is that he is a Tottenham Hotspur fan!

12

21 AND TAPS

Homeboys tradition was to warm up with a game of 21. This moved on to a game called *Taps* that was introduced to us by a friend of Tum's from the UK. Taps was one of the reasons we were so good. I will explain why shortly, after explaining the rules of 21. 21 is a common basketball variation usually played by at least three players on a half-court. The game is individual- ly-based and the object is to score exactly 21 points before your opponents. By individual, I mean you do not have any teammates within the game and you are responsible solely for your points and overall performance, while other players are attempting the same.

The game doesn't have a time limit and in order to win, you must score exactly 21 points. If you exceed that scoring limit, your score is reduced as a penalty. Some rules are universally applied, while other rules are loosely interpreted based on the group of players with which you are playing.

Basic rules of 21

A three-point shot earns you three points.

Regular shots made inside the three-point line are worth two points.

Free throws made from the free-throw line are worth a point.

That's the gist of it. So, before our weekend games, we would play 21 as a warm up and the winner would get first pick when choosing teams, the runner-up would get second pick.

Taps was a much tougher game and required more skill. The main difference was in the points. A regular shot was worth a point, and a three-pointer was worth two. In 21, when you score a regular shot, you take three free throws, each worth a point. However, in Taps, you had to take a three-point shot and this was still worth a point.

Understandably, people who have never played basket- ball or who don't know the rules may find this confusing, but the point I am bringing home is that every player had to master the art of a three-point shooting.

In conclusion, every single Homeboys player was good at a three-point shooting and since Taps and 21 were indi- vidual games, we all had to master the art of rebounding and defending.

This was the reason even without a coach, we would terrorise other neighbourhood teams and our stamina was relentless.

⓭

GAMES TO REMEMBER

There were so many games that I played in but some I remember like it was yesterday. The joy, the excitement, the adrenalin rush!

The first one was a three-or-three tournament at the former Yugoslavian embassy. The host was Sugar Shack Sounds. I remember deciding to enter even though our chances were slim, it was Kazhila, Mumba, Inncocent, Kennedy, and myself. We were going up against seasoned professionals in this tournament and Kazhila didn't have a pair of sneakers that day, he had to borrow them from an opponent, Kevin Kaswilo. When his team was playing, he would be in his slops and Kazhila would give him back his sneakers when it was his team's turn to play. Not to forget Robert Moyo, our reliable supporter who passed away in 2017, a day before my birthday.

It was a round-robin tournament with a prize for the winners and the runners up. We won all our games and reached the semi-finals. We were complete, total underdogs and since everyone loved the Cinderella story, the crowd was supporting us. I guess that's what fuelled us on and as unlikely as it would seem, we reached the finals.

The tournament favourites were made up of Fred Kansuma aka Slim (also a Makeni resident), Joel Chibanga aka Jay Bull, and Alan Shawa. These people were seasoned veterans and I remember Slim telling me that if we can reach the final, there is no way we were going to beat them. We even had a side bet, that was how confident he was.

We played our hearts out but we could not cross the final hurdle. We came second, which was a milestone for five teenagers from a farm area, one of them playing with borrowed sneakers!

The prize money was handed out at a prize giving cere- mony later that night, and I went up to receive it. I was proud of our hard work. Outside the hall, we decided to count the money for us to split it, Robert was the most excited of us all even though he was more like a mascot than a player. We counted our winnings and the cash was short. Thank God, we had decided to count it before we left. I went back in screaming, "We've been short changed! We've been short changed!" Obviously, the organisers didn't believe us but they ended up giving in and handed us the shortfall. What a day!

Another famous and memorable tournament was called *the Namwianga invitational*. What made this special was that it was on my old-stomping ground,

Namwianga Chris- tian Secondary School, in the tiny town of Kalomo.

This trip was made up of The Homeboys as well as some other players we teamed up with, namely: Levy Ngulube, Kevin Kaswilo, Kwayo, and Chisha. We had hooked up with these people when we played in Matero and decided to register for the tournament. From the Homeboys' side, it was Mumba, Inncocent, Kennedy, and myself. We used train from Lusaka to Kalomo, which normally should take thirteen hours, but it can take longer hours due to unforeseen circumstances. This time around, our faithful supporter, who was our motivator, was not with us – he is in a resting place. However, we recruited a new supporter, Frasier Mwansa Kapenda aka Mr Operator. He used to be my senior at College in Chingola and we met up in Lusaka some weeks before the tournament. I told him about it and he didn't hesitate and came along for the adventure.

It was a long trip, yet a mile a minute because of our number. There were about nine or ten teams participating and we steam-rolled them all. It was great hearing my former teachers in the background commenting about how I was so tiny at school (actually, I was cut from the first team in Grade 10 due to my size). Now here, I am helping to beat every team that came along.

To cut the long story short, for that tournament, we had no competition at all; it was like bringing the Chicago Bulls of the Jordan era to play against high school teams in Zambia. We were overwhelming favourites, and we proved it by lifting the trophy.

After the tournament, it was time to head back to Lusaka, trophy in hand. We waited for hours for the train, but none of us cared. We were the champions! Frasier entertained us every step of the way. He was a clown! Because of mechanical issues, the train dropped us off in Choma and we decided to hitchhike back to Lusaka. After several rides, we dropped off in Makeni around 21:00. We had five cottages at home that my mum used to rent out and one of them was vacant at the time, and I offered my mates some mattresses from my house to camp out in the cottage instead of them travelling late at night. I told mum about our victory and my sugges- tion and she was thrilled. We talked and talked throughout the night and the next morning, everyone headed home. Of course, Ken decided to be the first to have the trophy; we chose to share it over the course of the year.

Playing in an area called *Matero* was next on our list. There was no specific game but this is where we met some of our future teammates at a ZBA team called *Matero Magic*.

Matero is a township in the North-Western part of Lusaka. Curiosity and adventure made us go there. The courts were of a good standard even though the rims were much higher than normal. The main memory of Matero was one of the Sundays that we decided to go and play there. We used public transport, a mini bus, from Makeni to Kulima Tower (this was one of the main bus stops/ranks in the Lusaka Town Centre), from there we took another bus to Matero. It was Ken, Innocent, Mumba, and myself. I had a spare pair of sneakers that I lent to Mumba for the day and after the game, he put them in a plastic bag and put his shows back on.

We got onto the bus from Matero to Kulima Tower and as we were getting on the bus to Makeni, someone snatched the bag with my sneakers out of Mumba's hand. I think it was the adrenalin rush but all four of us jumped up and gave chase! After the thief realised that he was being chased after, he dropped one sneakers on the ground. Two minutes later into the chase, he dropped the plastic with the other sneaker in it. "You guys are crazy," he shouted in our local language.

What is shocking is that even after we had a four-hour game, we still had the energy to chase after a thief in the centre of Lusaka town. After the incident, we got back into the bus, laughing all the way back to Makeni.

Other places that spring to mind were Munali and Evelyn Hone College (both the indoor and the outdoor courts) and meeting several interesting characters. There was a guy whom we all used to call *Adihash*. I have no idea why that name, but his name just stuck. So we played in every region of Lusaka, north, south, west, and east.

Next up were two games I will never forget. The local derby against a group of guys from the other side of Makeni and a game against the Makai brothers and their new team in Lusaka West.

I will start with the Makeni derby. When it comes to this game, think of Orlando Pirates versus Kaizer Chiefs, Liverpool versus Everton, or the LA Lakers versus the LA Clippers. One day, people from the east of Makeni showed up at the Islamic Court without notice or invitation. It was on a weekday and we were playing our usual game of Taps. The entrance to the Islamic Centre is quite a distance to the basketball court and you can see someone approaching the court from afar. One of us asked, "Who the heck is that?" There were about nine or ten hulks walking up to the court, three of them carrying basketballs and the others chanting some crazy tune. I recognised one of them, Grant Tuta. He was my mum's Goddaughter's son and three of his brothers went to Namwianga. This team came with no prior agree- ment and literally just came unannounced to challenge us on our own turf. Who were we to say 'no'!

It must have been overconfidence because we lost that game. Well, we didn't just lose it, we lost badly! After they left, we sat down in a circle licking our wounds, wondering what had just happened. The mighty Homeboys had been well and truly humbled. We started plotting revenge and as they say, "Revenge is sweet!"

A month or so after that defeat, we did exactly what the Makeni East guys did to us. They used to play at ZAMIM, a college further South of Lusaka that I had once attended. We showed up unannounced and challenged them on their turf! As Kennedy would say, "It was bloodshed!" This meant that we left no stone unturned, we walloped them so badly that we even started doing Harlem Globetrotter tricks. Like I said earlier, "Revenge is sweet!"

The Makai brothers and the Lusaka West team, we were all looking forward to this game. Lusaka West was a farm area and there was no easy way to get there using public transport. Evans organised a small car and seven of us crammed ourselves in it to make our way for a much-antici- pated game against our former teammates. Evans, Kennedy, Innocent, Mumba, Kazhila, myself, and two other players made up our team. Brian, Kozhi, and Victor made up theirs, the only other player I can remember was Chizola whom I used to play with at Namwianga, and it was good to see him. But once the game started, all pleasantries went out of the window.

It was a very tight and hard-fought game… tempers were flaring. I will never forget this game because we had decided to play a points' target and not using a time limit. We were trading basket for basket and after they had scored to tie up the game, we called a timeout. We made the play, I was given the task of taking the shot, score, and we win. Miss and it gives them the opportunity to go to the court and win. It was such a well-rehearsed move and I was given the ball at my favourite scoring position, at the right-hand corner of the free-throw line. I took the shot, it wasn't the cleanest shot I have ever taken but the follow-through was enough and I got the shooter's roll. It felt like time stood still as the ball rolled slowly round the rim and eventually went in. Evans went crazy, I just lifted my arms up and turned to face the crowd, the rest of the guys came to lift me up, screaming, "LIMBA!" Oh, what a day and a game those were.

14

OTHER BASKETBALL ADVENTURES

Apart from the exploits of the Homeboys, I have been a member of several other teams. I started playing basketball at ISL and used to play a game every break time. Break was twenty-five minutes but that was more than enough time to shoot some hoops. The main players at this time were Kalolo Musonda (we used to argue over who was the *REAL* Kal), Mwombecki Semiti, Yusuf Bhana, George Greggory, Maano Obeysekere, others and myself. We used to play after school as well. At the time, when I was there, ISL was not well known for its sports, and basketball was way down on the pecking order. However, the one time we held a tournament was one of the most significant moments in my early life.

Our school team was so dysfunctional that we did not even have a jersey; we all wore different t-shirts. We were the only school to do that despite being the school where all the supposed rich kids went. My brother and his girlfriend at the time, Mwangala, came to watch.

Unsurprisingly, we dumped out in the first round but a team that caught my eye were wearing a yellow jersey with the name *Cobras* on it. I recognised Evans on that team and they also had an American player by the name of *Moon Blanton* and an amazing player by the name of *Godson Simakomo*. They also had Emmanual Bwalya Sampa (now known as Miles, the current Mayor of Lusaka). I was in awe of this team as they blew everyone away and lifted the trophy. They had a play called *Gorilla* and it would just bamboozle opponents. They were unstoppable and I would do anything to join them.

As ISL was not a traditional secondary school, my mum took the decision of looking for a traditional boarding school for me. We tried a few, including Mpelembe (where my brothers went) in Kitwe and St Paul's in Kabwe. Even- tually, we tried Namwianga in Kalomo and I got accepted. Deep down, this was my dream because all I could think of was the yellow jersey with the name Cobras on it. All I could think of was Moon Blanton and his American accent. Leaving ISL was easier than I thought. I had been there since Grade 1 but most of my close friends moved on while I was still there. I guess the excitement and anticipation of going to a basketball giant of a school made my move much smoother.

Boarding school life was completely different to what I thought, from the food to the ablution facilities. But one thing that was great was the basketball. Namwianga was a Church of Christ Mission School and had an American influence, hence the basketball. There were three courts, which were very uncommon for a Secondary School in Zambia but the most alluring thing was that the courts had floodlights! No Secondary School court of that time had floodlights. This meant we could train during the day as well as at night or early morning.

Evans welcomed me on my first day. I travelled to Kalomo by the bus with my mum's business partner, Emmanuel Bwalya. He and my mum had a company called *Kenge* that used to manufacture liquid washing detergent. He took me all the way to the school and made his way back to Lusaka after making sure that I was in safe hands. Evans was a celebrity at the time, a guy from Lusaka, a basketball player and his dad was well-known in the Southern Province. He walked up to meet me with a portable cassette recorder in his hand and Tracy Chapman playing on it. He introduced me to his crew, that would soon be mine. Chizola Daka, Absalom Banda aka Bisa and the late Marston Musokot- wane (he passed away this year, 2021).

I was thirteen years of age, the youngest in Grade 10 and my first night in Boarding School was traumatic to say the least. A majority of students were much older than I was and my Nyanja speaking skills were not the best, having been at ISL since Grade 1 and was only speaking English at home. Eventually, I settled in and made some other good friends along the way. Bruce Kakompe Mulyata, who wasn't a basketball player but was given the job of a scorekeeper. Also, I made friends with three guys who were a grade behind me, mainly because of our age and another reason was that they had been cut from the team by the new Coach who had just come back from America, Lovemore Sikaale. The names of the guys were Caesar Cheelo, Bright Mwewa, and Franklin Wood (whose dad was a missionary teacher from America). One of the benefits of being friends with Franklin was that we were allowed to have lunch/supper at his house at times. Indeed, that was a great treat!

Also, I forged a strong friendship with Lloyd Moonga, Chaishaba Masengu, and Samson Mujuda.

Back to the basketball... Grade 10 and my first year at Namwianga, in 1989, was not great in terms of basketball. I was cut from the team due to my size and was told by Coach Sikaale to try again next year. I worked my butt off and was selected for the team the same year. I missed the schools' national tournament but at least I did get to don the famous Cobra's jersey that year.

The next year, 1990, was much better for me at Namwi- anga. I was familiar with boarding school's life and was now back in the team one hundred per cent. We played several games against Hillcrest in Livingstone, Choma Secondary had Collins Kaswilo in the team, Kevin's brother who would later become my teammate, Monze Secondary had a giant of a player called *Phillip Gander*, and the local derby against Kalomo Secondar had Victor Mukupa, a former Namwianga student and had two brothers, John and Orgency. We also travelled to Lusaka for the Kabulonga invitational tournament.

However, the most emotional and unforgettable tour- nament of that year was the 1990 Senior Schools National Basketball Championships held at Canisius Secondary School in Chisekese, a tiny town in the Southern Province even smaller than Kalomo. After schools had closed for the term, we stayed on for a week to train and prepare for the Nationals. In our first game, we played against a team from the Copperbelt and even though we won, Coach Sikaale was not impressed. This was mainly because one player, Godson, scored all our points for that game. The next game, we played more of a team game and I even got on the scoresheet when I played. The semi-finals was against a team called *Mukuba* from Kitwe in the Copperbelt. This team had two players who used to play professional basketball for one of the teams in Kitwe They were in their mid-twenties but had the build of thirty year olds! The only thing was that

Mukuba was a two-man team and as long as you took those two out of the game, then they were toothless. That is exactly what we did and we qualified for the final against Munali Secondary from Lusaka.

Now this was a team of note, Billy Banda, Tito Theyo, Pierra Phiri, and Lombe Chitambala. These guys were strong, tall, fast, and they had the perfect team.But, we ran them close and they didn't expect that. We were up by one with ten seconds to go. It was Munali's ball and it was inbound to Lombe. He went up for the shot and was fouled. Time was up, he had two shots on the free-throw line. All the players were moved off the court. It was just Lombe and the referee. If he made the first shot, scores would be even. If he made the next one, Munali would be crowned champions. He had all the time in the world, he took it and scored the first shot. Scores were even, but if he missed the next one, we would go to overtime.

I couldn't bear to watch, but just as he was about to take the shot, I opened them only to see the ball going swish into the hoop. Munali were champions, we had lost. I couldn't help myself and burst into tears, I was only fourteen years old, surrounded by people much older than I was. Every member of the Cobras was distraught and inconsolable. Coach Sikaale gave us words of encouragement, though. No one expected us to reach the final. Favourites were the hosts, Cannisuis as well as Mukuba, so to get that far and to lose by that slim margin was really something.

We received the second-prize trophy and made our way to our homes, the Lusaka guys to the North and the South- ern-Province people back to the South. I travelled with Godson, Evans, Chizola and a few others by the train. Sadly, this was my first and last National tournament because the following year, there were no sponsors and the event could not take place. Also, we were in our final year and many of us decided to put basketball aside for the last two terms and concentrate on our studies.

In 1991, after completing my Grade 12 at Namwi- anga, I stayed home for over nine months while waiting for the results to be released by the Examinations Council of Zambia. During that time, as stated in Chapter 4, I spent my days playing golf at home and basketball wher- ever I could. When the results were released, I applied for a scholarship at the Chingola School of Accounts in the Copperbelt Province aka Accountancy Training College and was accepted. This college was sponsored by ZCCM (Zambia Consolidated Copper Mines, the last company that my late father worked for and where my elder sister worked). It was a fully-sponsored scholarship; tuition fees, food, accommodation, and stationery were paid for. We received a bi-monthly (twice a month) allowance and a book allowance. These privileges were to die for, we were up-to-date with all the latest textbooks and exercise books. The book allowance was an additional form of a pocket money for all the students.

Chingola is a very small town and I soon discovered that there was a ZCCM-sponsored basketball team just a walking distance from the College (as most things in Chingola were). I found out there was a senior by the name of *Mwenya Munkonge* at the college, who was a member of the team (Nchanga Basketball). I, still being in love with basketball, approached him and asked what the procedure was. He told me that it was coming to practice, as long as the coach can see that you can bounce a basketball and make a layup, you are in.

And that was that, the next training session, I met my future teammates and I was in.

Our first major trip was to go for a tournament in Lusaka. I was so excited! We travelled by the bus and played in the two-day tournament. We did not farewell at all and we were knocked out in the first round. We were meant to head back to Chingola on Sunday, but there was a mix up with our transport, so we ended camping in one of the boardrooms at the ZCCM Head Office, where my sister, Priscilla, worked. This was during the time before cell phones were popular and easy to access, so she had no idea that I was in Lusaka. I went to her office and she was shocked to see me. Her first thought was that I had gone AWOL from college. I explained to her that we had come for a basketball tournament and we were stranded due to poor logistics. She was in the PR department and made a few calls and the next day, we had another bus ready to take us back to Chingola. This story doesn't have a lot of basketball in it, in fact, it carries a good fond memory that I was able to see my sister.

Unfortunately, I failed my first year at Chingola School of Accounts and lost my bursary. My only consolation was that four others didn't make it through and we ended up together at a College in Lusaka by the name of *ZAMIM*. My elder brother, Clement, had attended this school after Grade 12. It was based in the industrial area of Lusaka and had boarding rooms in an area called *Chilanga*, past Makeni. Kalolo, my friend from ISL, was also at ZAMIM and soon enough, I was drafted into the college-basketball team.

There was no league for colleges and we pretty much used to attend friendly games against another private college called *ZIBC*. **ZIBC** was based at the Zamsure Sports Complex and they had an indoor court. At the time, ZAMIM had no court either at the campus in town or at the boarding campus in Chilanga. We just put together all the people who could play and arranged for the bus so we could play against ZIBC.

My first game was a success as I was a virtual unknown and as usual, due to my height and glasses, people underes- timated me. I remember after the game being surrounded by people in the bus, everyone saying, "Wow! We had no idea you could play. You are really good!"

The next game we played against ZIBC was a disaster. Before the game even started, we were warming up and I faked one of the guys who didn't take it too kindly. He stuck out a leg and I fell over it. My head hit the concrete. WHAM! As I got up, I felt stars in my eyes and the whole place went silent with others holding their mouths and eyes wide with shock. I did not feel any pain and blood started to drop down my shirt. I went to the bathroom, looked in the mirror and only then did I realise why their faces were etched with both sympathy and astonishment. My lip was five times its size, and my front tooth had pushed in. That was definitely game over for me. I got a lift home from a friend, George Mufana, who also attended ZAMIM and lived in Makeni. He wasn't a player but would always come along to watch.

I didn't need stitches and the dentist said my tooth would naturally push itself back into its natural position. I still have the battle scar on my lip, and guess what, the dentist was wrong; my tooth is still a bit pushed in and I have a small gap in my front teeth because of it.

My final remembrance was from ZAMIM but this was a game against the University of Zambia Pacers

(UNZA Pacers). This team was a ZBA team, part of the league and miles ahead of us. My friend, Nicholas, was part of this team as was Collins Kaswilo, Kevin's brother. Another former teammate was Miles Sampa from Namwianga. The Pacers underestimated us so much so that they felt we should play against the Lady Pacers, as it would be too much of a mismatch against them. They were wrong because I brought my A-game to UNZA that day!

I can't really remember who arranged for that game but it was set to be played on a Saturday. I was now in boarding at the Zamim campus in Chilanga and was quite a regular at the club with my college mates. The night before was like any other Friday at the clubhouse, but I left a bit earlier than usual because I was reminded that I had a game the next day. Zamim had no recognised coach and we went with the flow when playing. We also didn't have a team jersey, it was agreed that we all put on black t-shirts to at least have some form of a uniformity.

We arrived at the UNZA courts on a Saturday morning and started to warm up. I saw Nicholas, Collins, and Miles and said, "Hi." Nick being my close friend was not as arro- gant as the rest of his teammates. The game itself was mostly a back-and-forth affair with Kalolo and myself as the main scorers. I remember going to the scoreboard just to check the score in the second half and one of the scorekeepers telling me, "That's enough now, haven't you scored enough?" The Pacers could not believe that we were matching them but eventually, we ran out of steam and they won the game by two or three baskets. We received a standing ovation and I was given the nickname "Olajuwon" by one of the ZAMIM guys. They were so happy with that nickname that I didn't have it in my heart to disappoint them and tell them that I was a shooting-point guard and the real Olajuwon was a seven-foot (2.13 metres) tall Centre. I was more like a Spud Webb or Garry Payton but I don't think any of them knew who they were.

We headed back to campus having lost the game but gained the respect and the hearts of UNZA.

15

LONDON, ENGLAND

In 1995, after completing my AAT (Association of Accounting Technicians) qualification at ZAMIM, mum wanted me to go and study in the UK. I found a college called *Accountancy Tutors* in London and mum duly paid the fees. We arranged with Tum, who was in London that I would move in with him since he was staying in a two-bedroom flat. So, there was more than enough room. Tum and his brother, Sinjani, were working in London. Our plan was not a very good one because instead of applying for a student visa, we took it for granted that Zambia was a Visa-free country and we could just enter and leave the UK as we pleased. Bags packed, pocket money in hand, we went to the airport with Mum, Clement, and Robert to see me off. We said our goodbyes and off I went on my next big step.

Apparently, as I was in the plane, there was an announce- ment by the UK government that Zambian citizens were now required to apply for Visas (workers, visitors, and students). The flight was with KLM and we passed through Malawi, then Kenya. We stopped in Holland to change planes and after a two-hour wait, we were off to Heathrow. Tum had told me what to do when I got there but unfor- tunately, I was detained by the immigration officials who asked me for my visa. When I said I didn't have one, they said that I was ignorant and that they would not allow me in. I was crestfallen, but eventually after about three hours of being grilled, I was let in temporarily. I met up with Tum at the Tube station and instead of going home, he took me to his favourite pub, suitcases and all! It was a Friday night, so why not!

Due to the confusion with the visa, I did not manage to complete my CIMA (Chartered Institute of Management Accountants) in England and was informed that I would need to go back to Zambia and apply for a Visa in order to go back. My Visa was declined, stating the fact that there were enough colleges in Zambia offering CIMA, therefore, there was no need for me to go to the UK for that.

Mum decided to enroll me at NIEC School of Business Management in Ndola and I spent the rest of 1995 there in boarding.

16

GOODBYE ZAMBIA

n February 28, 1999, I left Zambia to start a new life in South Africa. Mukumbi Kafuta, a close friend from ZAMIM had moved to Johannesburg the year before and Robert had followed suit. It was a tough decision and it is only now that I realise it was the right one. Basketball was no longer one of my priorities, and alcohol and cigarette smoking had taken over. By the time I got on that luxury coach heading for South Africa, all that was on my mind was getting a job and having fun with Mukumbi and Robert. I have been to the UK before, so when we arrived at Park Station in the Central of Johannesburg, it was not as WOW as what other first-time visitors to South Africa might feel. Robert was there to meet me and we got onto a taxicab to what would be my home for the next two years. The name of the complex was Bridgetown in the suburb of Bloubosrand, near Fourways. Robert told me that there were other guys living in the tiny three bedroom unit. In total, there was Mukumbi, Robert, Kalaba, Kaemba, Honest (Mukumbi's brother Kyala aka Quick would join 3 or so months later), and myself, making it seven of us in a tiny three bedroom with only two of us working.

At first, it was a great time but soon the money that I had come with from Zambia ran out and we were still jobless. From having three meals a day, we could only manage two – breakfast and supper. We could only eat breakfast if we sold some of the 1.5 litre-coke bottles to the local tuck shop. From these sales, we would manage to get a half loaf and share that between the five of us. We would then wait for Mukumbi and Kaemba to get home before we could all eat supper together.

In-between the job hunting, an old passion was reig- nited. Bridgetown had a basketball court on the grounds and one day I took a walk there and found some guys playing. There was Dennis, the dreadlocked Malawian, Tony and his younger brother, Shingi, and a guy who I became close to by the name of Mongezi. We would play every after- noon, especially when these guys had a day off from work. Mongezi though was like me. He was not working, so we would spend most of the day playing basketball. Out of the guys I was staying with, only Kalaba could play but others would tag along and they were so impressed as only Mukumbi and Robert knew my talents.

Job-hunting was getting very frustrating. However, as I was contemplating looking for a club to join, I received my first-temporary job offer. Needless to say, basketball took a back seat again and the drinking and smoking came back into the equation. I got my first job in September, 1999. The next time I would shoot a basketball would be in 2017, almost twenty years later, at a court in Randburg, which was not far from where my son would go for soccer practice.

When I left Bridgetown, I never saw Tony, Shingi, Dennis or Mongezi again. Of my Bridgetown crew, only Kaemba and Honest still live in South Africa. Robert and Quick passed away, Kalaba and Mukumbi went back to Zambia.

17

THE LOVE OF MY LIFE

I met my wife, Sheba, at a local restaurant called *Fine Foods*. The owners were the tenants at her mum's house and she would pass the time there with the nieces and sister of Mrs Kay (as the owner was affectionately called). I had been in Ndola for most of that year, 1995, and when I got back to Lusaka, the first thing I was told by the guys was that there was a new restaurant in town and there were some smoking hot girls mostly. Mrs Kay was a former student at Mpelembe hence she knew my brother, Clement. Sheba also attended Mpelembe, albeit at much different periods than Mrs Kay and my brother. We were frequent patrons at Fine Foods and Sheba and I discovered we had a lot in common. We both loved to read, we loved music, and we loved watching movies. I never once made a move on her since I was too focused on the alcohol and having a good time with my crew. I know this is swaying from basketball but this is a period in my life where the basketball took a back seat. We would play occasionally but first priority would be drinking, Fine Foods, party, and disco.

Sheba and I ended up being quite close and we would exchange novels, music, and movies. I would advise her against certain guys and she would escort me to go and see my girlfriends.

In 1996, my mum encountered financial difficulties and I could not continue with my studies. It was decided that I should start looking for a job with the current qual- ifications that I had. In those days, you could not e-mail your CV, you had to go in person to a company and hand it in or post it. Things were tough and my days were spent at home or, once in a while, we would play basketball with the guys but not to the extent that we used to.

My lucky break came when my childhood friend, Chola Folotiya, offered me a job. Chola and I had been friends from ISL but he had left around Grade 5 or 6 to go and study in the UK. We would always get together when he came back for summer holidays and would interchange weekly between my house and his. He was short-sighted like I am and had started wearing glasses from a younger age like I did. People used to think we were twins. As we grew older, however, our passions changed and I got more and more into basketball of which he was never a player or a fan. He was more of a rugby player.

My brother, Tulani, passed away a few weeks before Chola came home to pay his respects. After the usual pleas- antries, he asked me what I was up to. I told him that I had done my accounting and was looking for a job. Chola's dad was also the late and he had left his businesses to his kids. Chola had taken over the bar but had changed it to an appliance shop and a makeup and cosmetics shop. He offered me to come and work with him albeit at a low salary but at least it would give me the chance to learn in the work environment.

I worked with Chola for about nine months until his accounting software consultant, Boaz, came to do a consul- tation one day. After talking for a bit, I learned that his younger brother had attended Namwianga. The next time he came to the office, he asked me if I would be interested in getting a fulltime position at one of the big and emerging companies. "Of course, I would be interested!" He sent me the details and I went for my interview at Zambeef. This was all with Chola's blessing and he was both thrilled and excited for me. I got the job as an Assistant Accountant at the Zambeef Head Office in Kabulonga.

After a few months of working, the Financial Controller asked if I knew anyone else who would be interested in a job. The company was growing at a rapid rate and needed more hands on deck. Robert had recently lost his job at Pamodzi Hotel, so he was the first person that came to mind. Lo and behold, he got the job and we worked together for the next year or so.

In-between all of this, Sheba and I were still friends. She came to drop off a Babyface tape at the cosmetics shop once and Chola was like, "Wow! You have a good taste in girls!" I told him that we were just friends, but he refused because somehow, he was convinced otherwise by the way she looked at me.

After numerous "not so serious" relationships, I finally got the courage to ask Sheba out. We went to a place called *Patello's* with Mumba and Mailon Moono and their girl- friends. I remember that after dropping her at her gate with the minibus we had hired for the day, I asked for my first kiss and she said no. She gave me a peck on the lips and that was how it all began.

Unfortunately, the sooner had it started, the sooner it came to a halt as I made the decision to relocate to South Africa. We promised to keep in touch and we had a long-dis- tance romance from February, 1999, up until 2002, when she left Zambia and joined me in South Africa. We got engaged in December 2003 and set our wedding date for December, 2005.

We got married in Lusaka on the 17th of December, 2005, at Pamodzi Hotel. It was a great ceremony and one I will never forget. Our MC was hilarious and everything went quite smoothly apart from Robert and his usual drunk antics, which people found almost as hilarious as the MC. My wife has given me three beautiful kids, namely; Grace, Malaika, and my son Kalenga Junior. My little family keeps me going, and it has been with me through my diabetes scare in 2014 up until now that I have decided to become a writer. I love them all dearly.

18

CONCLUSION AND QUOTES

The basketball journey and passion are what I will never forget. From watching our first NBA videos with my brother and his friends, then inviting my friends over to watch the same videos (Larry Bird, Magic Johnson, Michael Jordan in his early years at the Chicago Bulls) to playing games across the city of Lusaka. Innovation to make sure we had a court, carrying hand pumps to the court with three flat balls with no grip, pumping one after the other just to make sure we use as much time as we could and playing until sunset. Being belittled due to my height and spectacles and proving everyone wrong and that looks can be deceiving.

The perseverance was something else as well. We had no proper physios or doctors and the amount of times we had twisted ankles and still played on. 'Just bandage it up and soak it in hot water when you get home.' That was the mantra whenever someone had a swollen ankle or knee. For all we knew, there could have been ligament damage or something more serious! Swollen fingers from the ball hitting us right on the tip of the fingers, this was also a common place but did not deter us from playing.

For me, what basketball did was to keep me out of trouble, to keep me fit and enjoy myself while doing some- thing we all loved. Unfortunately, this all became too good to be true because bad habits took over and most of us started drinking alcohol and smoking. This took precedence over basketball and eventually Homeboys was no more. Instead of meeting on the court, we ended up meeting at bars and nightclubs.

I have not included other players in the body of this book. This is because I had never been to their house, I had no idea what their last name was and the only thing I knew is that they lived in Makeni and they played basketball. They are as follows:

1. Patrick Muyumu: A smooth player who would normally come to the court smelling of alcohol and cigarettes but would still play all the same.
2. Davie Mvula aka Catfish: I only put his full name because I only learned it this year via Facebook.
3. Fidelis: Another beer drinking, cigarette smoking player.

4. Tim: Fidelis friend so also beer drinker but not smoker, surprisingly.
5. Henry: Brian Makai's schoolmate.

I have no idea where all of these guys are apart from Catfish, we recently became friends on Facebook as mentioned.

My love for the game has never stopped and the house my family and I now live in has a basketball hoop just above the garage.

I would like to end this book with some quotes from the great Michael Jordan, who is in my opinion the greatest player the NBA(National Basketball Association) has ever had. .

- *I can accept failure, everyone fails at something. But I can't accept not trying*
- *I've missed more than 9000 shots in my career. I've lost almost 300 games. 26 times, I've been trusted to take the game winning shot and missed. I've failed over and over and over again in my life. And that is why I succeed.*

Well that is that. Thank you for sharing this amazing journey of growing up, basketball, and friendship.

PICTURES

Brian Makai, Evans Sodala and me in 1994

My brother Clement at the Makeni Ecumenical Centre

The Namwianga Cobras 1990

My family and family friends in Luanshya in 1980

Makeni Homeboys

The original Makeni Homeboys

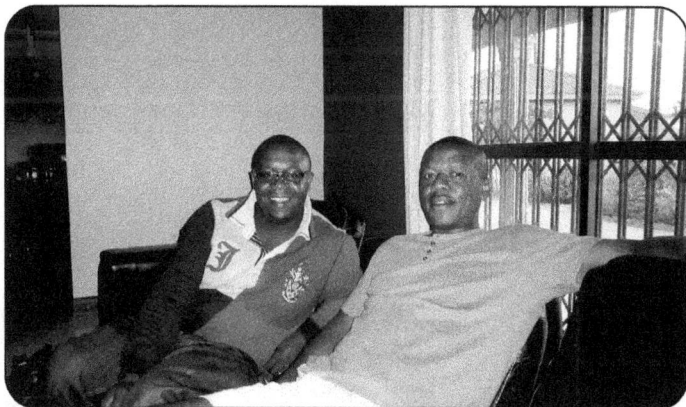

Wezi Mtonga and Kamima Nyirenda

**Brian Makai, Victor Makai and me
on our way to play basketball**

**Gershom Siame, Jones, the late Robert
Moyo and me outside Zambeef**

Evans Sodala (holding the ball) and me at Namwianga

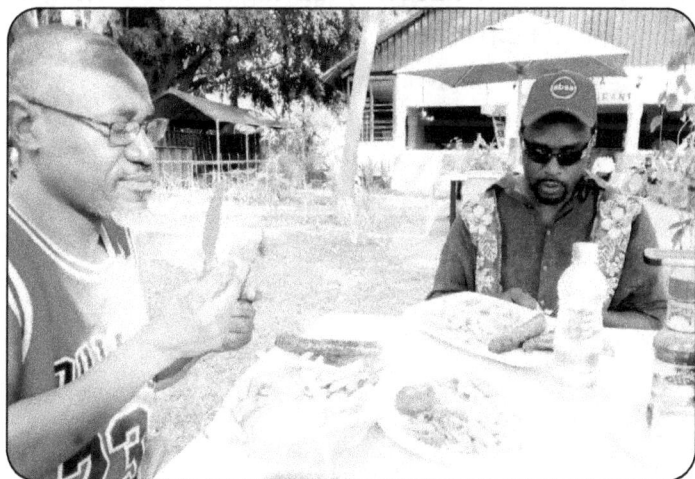

**Chizola Daka (former classmate and Namwianga
Cobra team mate) and the late Kennedy Kapaya
(in the dark glasses and cap, MHSRIP)**

Thank you for reading Makeni Homeboys. I hope you enjoyed it! Please let me know about what you thought about the book by leaving a short review, it will help other readers find the story.

www.ingramcontent.com/pod-product-compliance
Lightning Source LLC
Chambersburg PA
CBHW060036050426
42448CB00012B/3037